A WILTSHIRE CAMERA

A WILTSHIRE CAMERA

1835~1914

David Burnett

The Dovecote Press

First published in 1975 by
The Dovecote Press Ltd, Stanbridge, Wimborne, Dorset
Reprinted 1979, 1985

© David Burnett

ISBN 85955 017 6

Printed by Biddles Ltd, Guildford and King's Lynn

Contents

Acknowledgements

I am deeply indebted to the following for allowing me to make use of their photographs: The Wiltshire Archaeological Society: 13, 26, 30, 33, 48, 50, 56, 84, 92, 96, 100, 102, 116, 125, 127, 131, 141, 146; Salisbury and South Wiltshire Museum: 27, 38, 41, 58, 67, 68, 71, 72, 78, 91, 95, 115, 122, 129, 130, 137; 143; The Science Museum: 1, 28, 59, 61, 124, 126; Wiltshire Library and Museum Service, Swindon Divisional Library: 2, 8, 16, 35, 73, 83, 87, 88, 89, 103, 104, 105, 107, 109, 110, 112, 113, 136, Wootton Bassett Historical Society: 4, 29, 44, 70, 77, 80, 81, 90, 121, 147, 148, 150; Yelde Hall Museum, Chippenham: 12, 22, 37, 45, 128, 134, 142; Cricklade Historical Society: 20, 39, 63, 69, 98, 106; Calne Town Council: 6, 60, 85, 108, 117 (W. Lock), 119 (M. Maundrell); Wiltshire Library and Museum Service, Melksham Divisional Library: 9, 135, 138, 140; The Athelstan Museum, Malmesbury: 52, 62, 66; The Dewey Museum, Warminster: 11, 40, 45; Wiltshire Regimental Museum: 93, 97; The County Records Office, Trowbridge: 47, 57; The Women's Institute, Mere: 42, 132, 151; Aldbourne Photographic Club: 123, 144; Bradford-on-Avon Preservation Trust: 18; Wiltshire Newspapers, Swindon: 10, 133; C. & T. Harris (Calne) Ltd.: 51; The Marquess of Bath: 64; The Earl of Pembroke: 65; M. J. Lansdown and K. H. Rogers: 5, 7, 15, 17, 49, 86; Mrs H. N. Hooper: 32, 76, 114, 120, 149; L. Jukes: 14, 19, 23, 43, 46, 74; E. G. H. Kempson: 3, 55, 94, 139; S. Hudson: 21, 31, 34, 111; W. L. Standerwick: 99, 101; R. Lever: 54, 118; E. J. Sandell: 24, 53; Mr and Mrs E. W. Gye: 75, 79; A. Pitt-Rivers: 36, A. Riggs: 82; H. M. Trethowan: 25.

A large number of people have helped to make this book possible, and although my first debt is to those who provided the photographs, I would like to thank the following for their friendly and welcome assistance with the research: Ron Lever, Mrs Hooper, Mr and Mrs Gye, Mrs Nora Rutter (The Women's Institute, Mere), Miss N. M. G. Carter (Cricklade Historical Society), Miss K. A. MacKean (Bradford-on-Avon Preservation Trust), J. Ward (The Science Museum), W. L. Standerwick, R. Baggs (C. & T. Harris Ltd.), Maurice Crane (Aldbourne Photographic Society), M. Marshman (Melksham Divisional Library), Patrick Hillman (Amesbury Divisional Library), Roger Trayhurn (Swindon Divisional Library), M. S. Webb (Calne Town Council), L. Jukes, J. A. Chamberlain and C. J. Smith (Yelde Hall Museum, Chippenham), S. Hudson (The Athelstan Museum, Malmesbury), E. G. H. Kempson, E. J. Sandell, A. Riggs, A. Pitt-Rivers, H. M. Trethowan, Miss Austin (Librarian to Lord Bath), and P. Trollop (The Dewey Museum, Warminster).

I am particularly grateful for the help I received from K. H. Rogers of the County Records Office in suggesting many of the photographic sources; P. Gingell of Wootton Bassett Historical Society for the use of his extensive notes on the history of the town; Hugh de S. Shortt, Curator of Salisbury and South Wiltshire Museum for producing the endpapers; and R. E. Sandell, Librarian to the Wiltshire Archaeological Society, who provided a great deal of information about many of the photographs.

NOTE: Where two photographs are below each other the caption symbols ▽ and ◁ apply to the lower photograph. ▽ ▽

Introduction

Throughout the summer of 1835 a well-to-do English country gentleman with a taste for science and mathematics was busy at his home, Lacock Abbey, with what his wife Constance described as 'little mouse traps'. The man was William Henry Fox Talbot, and he was on the brink of producing the first photographic negative. The 'mouse traps' were box cameras fitted with lenses, each box containing a sheet of writing paper that had previously been bathed in a silver chloride solution.

The idea that chemicals could be used to preserve a photographic image had first come to this remarkable man, so uncharacteristic of his class and age, when he was holidaying beside Lake Como in 1833: 'How charming it would be if it were possible to cause these natural images to imprint themselves durably, and remain fixed upon the paper'. Within six years Fox Talbot had learnt how to produce positives, a discovery that was to change the entire course of photographic history as it meant that an unlimited number of prints could be made from one negative. In 1840 he invented the calotype. The development of the image became a dark-room process, and exposure times were reduced from thirty to two minutes. And in 1844 Fox Talbot published the first part of *The Pencil of Nature*, a book containing twenty-four calotype illustrations all taken at Lacock and outlining the various uses of photography. Large quantities of his other early negatives and prints lay hidden in a trunk in the attic at Lacock for nearly ninety years, until they were found in 1937 by his granddaughter Miss Matilda Talbot and presented to the Science Museum.

As the nineteenth century advanced the demand for photographs grew. The High Street photographer flourished: the triumphs and tragedies, celebrations and ceremonies, street scenes and market days that are the hallmarks of Victorian provincial life appeared now as ½d. postcards. By this means the hustle and bustle of Swindon, Trowbridge or any of the other manufacturing towns could be captured, printed, and shown to the most disbelieving and isolated of Salisbury Plain's shepherds. The railway fitter could come face to face with the Salisbury cleric, the Malmesbury publican with his Tisbury counterpart. Somehow the camera was able to throw a bridge over the barrier of chalk that had for so long separated the two halves of Wiltshire.

The motorcar has finished what the camera began. If the downs are no longer an obstacle to progress, the world they unconsciously secured no longer exists. Thanks to Fox Talbot and his successors, some of its images are preserved and we can turn back the pages on a Wiltshire that has changed more in the last sixty years than it had in six centuries.

1. The first photograph: William Henry Fox Talbot's negative of the inside of a lattice window in Lacock Abbey, taken in August 1835. The negative is its original size, and Fox Talbot mounted it on a card and wrote beside it: 'Lattice window (with the camera obscura) August 1835 – When first made, the squares of glass 200 in number could be counted with the help of a lens'.

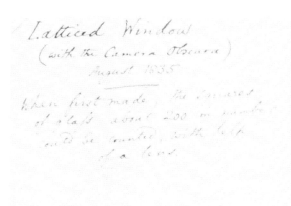

Towns and Villages

2. (*Overleaf*) Clappen's Corner, Swindon in 1904 when 4½ miles of tramways were opened with a maximum fare of 3d. Conductors were paid 4½d. an hour. On the day of the ceremonial opening the first tram to use the line rounded Clappen's Corner too fast and dislodged the trolley head: the town dignitaries were not amused when they had to dismount and board another tram. The trams were replaced by buses in 1929 and sold for £5 each.

4. Looking down through the centre of Clyffe Pypard towards the Church of St Peter in about 1890. The Goddard Arms is on the right.

3. Looking west down Marlborough High St. towards the Church of St Peter and St Paul in the summer of 1905. Writing of the High St. in 1907, A. G. Bradley remarked: 'The street is tilted sideways at such an angle, that the natives of rival Wiltshire towns, in their lighter moments, were accustomed to profess alarm at the prospect of encountering it in a two-wheeled trap'. This recaptures the tranquility of Wiltshire before the motor car.

5. The Market Cross, Castle Combe, in about 1895. Note the shield of the Tibetot family on the facing upright. The covered cross was regularly used by travelling tinkers to display their wares. The partially hidden horse-drawn bus used to travel twice a week to Bristol and Bath, and the passengers were compelled to dismount whenever a steep hill had to be climbed.

6. Looking up Calne High St. in about 1900. The decline of the wool trade 'was happily arrested by the Harris family of pork notoriety, and Calne is now the chief seat of that admirable product, Wiltshire bacon'.

8. The Chief Superintendent, Inspectors, Sergeants, and Constables of the Swindon Borough Force outside the County Constabulary in Eastcott Rd. in December 1911. Note that only 4 out of the 59 police officers in this photograph are without moustaches.

7. Melksham Fire Brigade fighting a fire at one of the cloth mills in about 1885.

9. Savernake Hospital, near Marlborough in 1905. The hospital was founded by subscription in 1866 and had beds for 21 patients. Outpatients paid 2s. 6d. a week, and the poor were given free treatment on the recommendation of a subscriber. This one small hospital served the medical needs of an area containing 40,000 people.

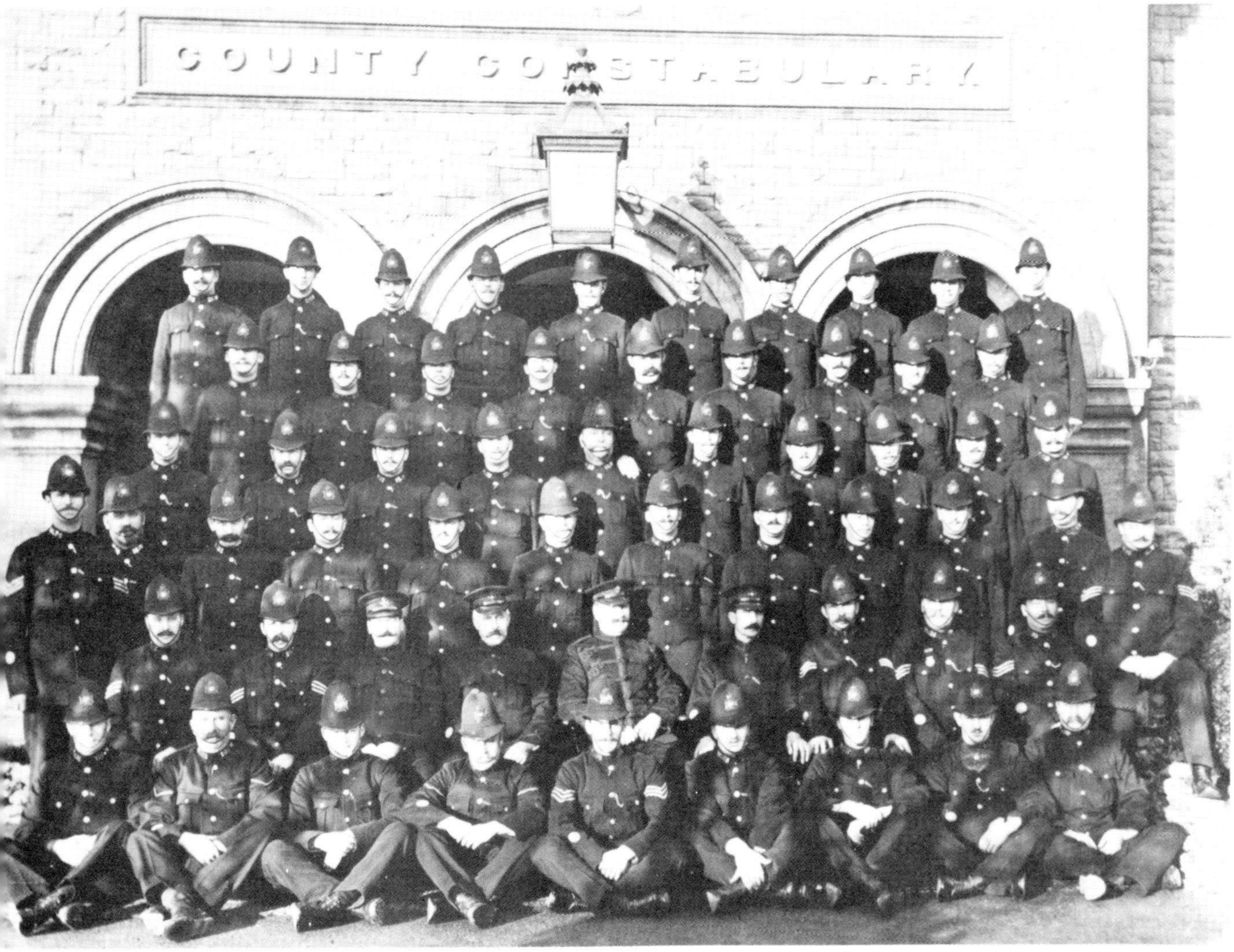
COUNTY CO STABULARY

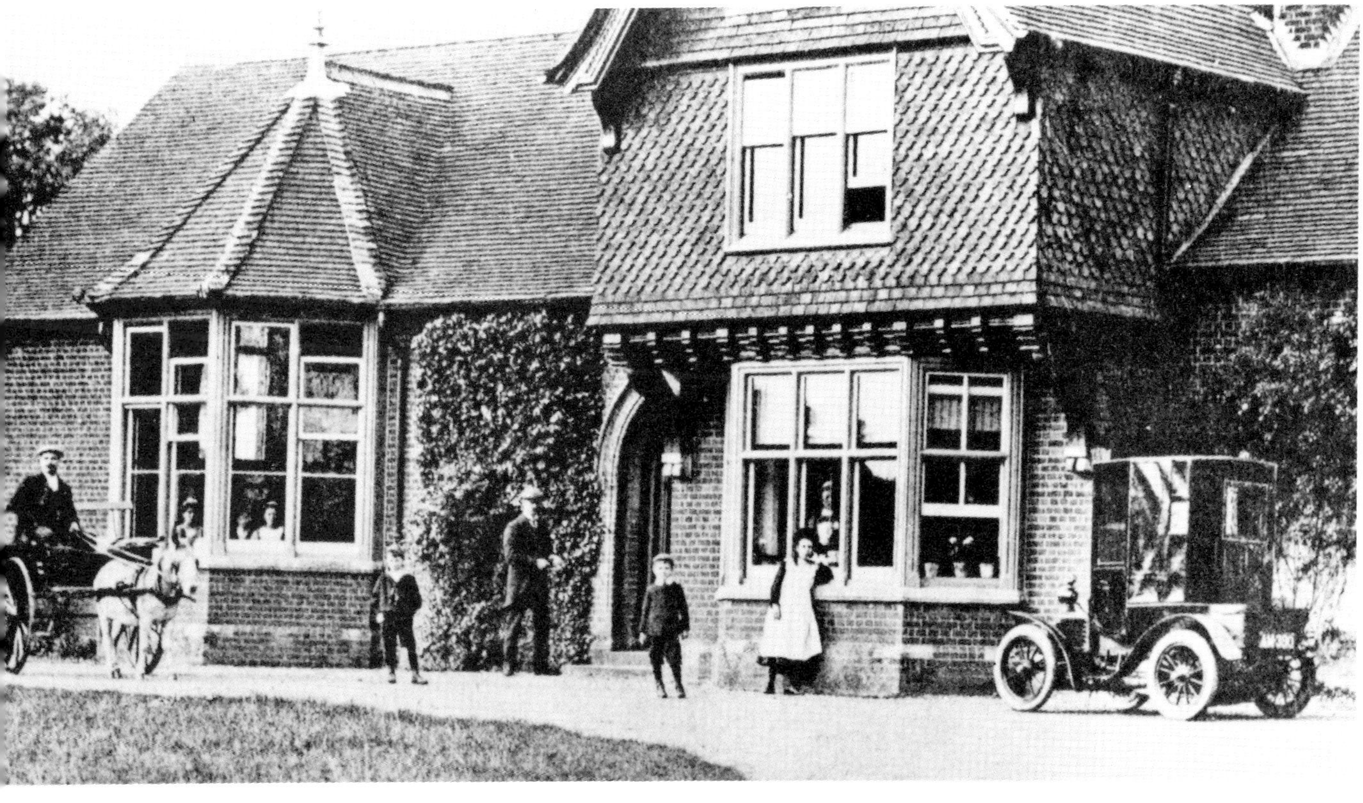

10. A Thursday market in Devizes, in about 1885. Note the carrier waggons in the foreground. In the days before motor transport the carrier was the sole link with the outlying villages. About 35 carriers operated out of Devizes on market day, two of them travelling as far as Salisbury – one via Warminster (30 miles), and the other via Shrewton (25 miles). Fares were about 2d. for parcels and 6d. for people, and the waggons averaged 7 m.p.h.

11. Looking down Warminster High St. in 1880. A cattle market is in progress, but the town was most famous for its corn market, which was once the biggest in the West of England.

12. Looking down Chippenham High St. in 1900 towards the old bridge over the Avon. The bridge was built in 1794 and a 19th century historian wrote about it: '. . . and when we consider it as being built at the expense of the Corporation and not of the county, we must allow it to reflect credit on the spirit and age when the improvement was made'. Alas, that same Corporation elected to demolish it in 1964.

13. Alton Barnes with the White Horse in the background in 1900. The White Horse was the creation of Robert Pile, the tenant at Manor Farm, who in 1812 hired a journeyman-painter called John Thorne to design the horse. Thorne undertook to do the job for £20 but having mapped out the figure and employed workmen to cut the turf he vanished with the money.

15. The Conigre pump, Trowbridge, some time before mains water was brought into the town in 1873. Note the water carrier in the foreground.

14. Laying main drainage in Russell St., Wilton, in 1910. The work was carried out by Irish navvies who were paid 4d. an hour.

16. The County Electric Pavilion, an early Swindon cinem in 1910. Seats cost between 3 and 1s., and the week's 'continuous programme' included *The Still Alarm, Daughter of Dixie, Tragedy in Toyland, a White Rose of the Wilds.*

17. The village of Erlestoke on the edge of Salisbury Plain in about 1890. A village that all 19th century maps and directories spell as either Earlstoke or Earl Stoke.

18. The Shambles, Bradford-on-Avon in about 1900. Areas known as 'The Shambles' are quite common throughout Wiltshire and were once covered markets.

19. Floods outside John White's Family Grocer's, North St., Wilton, in 1914. All four of the South Wiltshire rivers, the Nadder, Wylye, Avon, and Bourne, flooded virtually every year until dredging and clearing took place after the Great War.

20. Cricklade High St. before the erection of the Jubilee Clock. This photograph is very typical of Wiltshire towns in the last decade of the 19th century. On the right is The White Hart, the main Posting Inn; and on the left is the town pump, the Medical Hall, and the Temperance Hotel. Note the gas lamps and the cobbled gutters.

21. Looking up Malmesbury High St. towards the Abbey in 1893. On the left is The Kings Arms whose corpulent licensee Henry Jones was so well known and was visited by the Prince of Wales.

22. Chippenham Fire Brigade with their manual Merryweather engine in the 1890s. The engine was acquired in the 1840s and not replaced until 1902. After that it disappeared and was found in the old gasworks in 1937.

23. The Wylye valley village of
Hanging Langford in 1887.

24. Salisbury St., Amesbury, in about 1905. In 1855 the town could support seventeen craftsmen
– 2 millers, 3 wheelwrights, a mason, 4 cobblers, 2 blacksmiths, a basketmaker, a watchmaker,
a tanner, harnessmaker, and maltster. By 1903 mass-production and the growth of centralised
industries had reduced this number to eight.

Worthies

⌂ 26. A travelling pedlar on the edge of Salisbury Plain in about 1900.

◁ 25. (*Overleaf*) James Lawes and his wife outside their cottage in retirement in about 1890. It is now widely believed that Lawes was the model for Caleb Bawcombe, the hero of W. H. Hudson's *A Shepherd's Life*, first published in 1910. Lawes began shepherding at the age of six on the downs near Martin – the southern village was moved into Hampshire in 1895. James Lawes's life is best summed up in the final sentence of Hudson's book: 'But if 'twas offered to me and I was told to choose my work, I'd say, give me my Wiltsheer Downs again and let me be a shepherd there all my life long.'

▷ 27. Mr Thomas Yeates truffle-hunting at Winterslow in 1910. The beechwoods on the light chalkland of S. Wiltshire are one of the main areas where truffles grow in this country. The truffles were sniffed out by dogs – the Wiltshire pack of truffle-dogs were a mixed breed of Russian and French poodle – between late September and March. The truffles were best just before Christmas when they were fully grown and held a scent that the dogs could pick up. The tubers grew a few inches below the ground, and although the record size for a single truffle was about 2 lb., a haul of 8 lb. of tubers would have been an excellent day's work.

28. The gamekeeper at Lacock Abbey in about 1844. The gun is probably a converted muzzle-loader. Richard Jefferies, who lived at Coate, near Swindon, described the keeper's relationship with his gun in *The Gamekeeper at Home*, first published in 1878, as follows: 'It has been his companion for so many years that it is not strange he should feel an affection for it; no other fitted the shoulder so well, or came with such delicate precision to the present position. It has become almost a portion of his body, answering like a limb to the volition of will without the intervention of reflection'.

29. A group of Wiltshire worthies alongside the Crimea Gun and under the Town Hall at Wootton Bassett in the 1870s. The Crimea Gun was a 38-pounder Russian field gun captured at Sebastopol and presented to the town by Lord Panmure. It was melted down in 1942 to assist in the war effort.

30. A group of cottagers near Devizes in about 1900. This is one of several photographs in the book taken by Arthur Mitchell of Long St., Devizes, who as Relieving Officer for the No. 1 Devizes District was responsible to the Board of Guardians for the running of the Workhouse. The photographs were pasted into an album with no information, and the album was eventually sent to Devizes Museum by Mitchell's daughter with instructions that it should be destroyed if not of interest. Yet Mitchell's photographs portray cottage life in Wiltshire at the turn of the century perhaps better than any others.

31. Three Malmesbury 'commoners' in the Triangle in about 1904. The 'Commoners of the King's Heath' are townspeople who can claim direct descent from those who fought alongside King Athelstan in the 10th century, and on marriage they are given a grant of allotment land.

32. The inmates of the Dauntseys Almshouses, West Lavington, in about 1900. From left to right they are: Mrs Hobbs – who lived to be 96; Mrs Still; possibly Martha Dark; Mr Baker – in th red waistcoat of the almsmen; and Mrs Smith. The women are holding posies of marigolds and pansies.

Occasions

33. (*Overleaf*) Professor William Gowland (*centre*) directing the righting of the leaning upright of the trilithon at Stonehenge, which had slipped in the 16th century and was only supported by the Blue Stone. The operation took six weeks in the autumn of 1901. Many of the stones were in danger of collapse, and two had fallen on the evening of the last day of the 19th century; an event which was interpreted as one of prophetic doom by the Ancient Druid Order. Stonehenge was auctioned by Sir Edmund Antrobus in 1915 and bought by Sir Cecil Chubb at the knock-down price of £6,600. He in turn presented it to the nation.

35. The junction of Wood St. and the High St., Swindon, decorated for Queen Victoria's Diamond Jubilee in 1897.

34. Malmesbury Corporation welcoming home the volunteers who had served in the Boer War at the Cross Hayes 1903.

36. The employees of the founder of modern archaeolog
General Augustus Henry Lane Fox Pitt-Rivers, excavat-
ing the northern ditch of Martin Down Camp in 1895.

37. Circus elephants in the River Avon above the old brid
at Chippenham in about 1906. Travelling circuses wer
common to all market towns in the days before televisi
and it is possible that the elephants belong to Sangers
Circus, which was started by James Sanger on a £10 dis
ability pension given to him after losing three fingers at
Trafalgar.

38. The blindfolded initiation of Stonehenge's owner Sir
Edmund Antrobus and others into the Most Ancient Dr
Order on the day of the summer solstice, 21 June 1906.
The Druid Order described Stonehenge as their 'most an
cient shrine', and their faith as 'as it was in the days of
Pelagrius, the Teacher of Bangor, and of the brothers of
Iona, Glastonbury, and Calne'. The initiation of Sir Ed-
mund was a major victory for the Druids who had beer
outraged five years earlier when he insisted they pay a
shilling each whenever they wished to use Stonehenge.

39. Mrs Freeth being baptised at Hatchetts in the Tham
near Cricklade in 1890. This was the last Baptist baptism
in the river, and one can only feel sympathy for those
taking part in what was obviously a local holiday and
public spectacle.

40. Walter Long, Minister for Agriculture, speaking outside Warminster Conservative Working Men's Club in 1913. Warminster was then overwhelmingly Liberal. The clock has been moved into the Bath Rd.

41. A Review of the Junior Sea Scouts in the Market Square, Salisbury in 1902 at the time of Edward VII's Coronation. The statue is of Sidney Herbert, War Minister during the Crimean War and Florence Nightingale's long-suffering patron and greatest admirer.

2. General Booth speaking in Mere in the early part of this century. William Booth was the founder of the Salvation Army, which by 1900 was feeding 21,000 people a day and had hostels and shelters throughout the world.

. Crowds waiting outside Wilton House, Wilton, for the arrival King Edward and Queen Alexandra when they stayed with e Earl of Pembroke in 1908. The man in the top hat was Mr. tty, a Boer War veteran.

44. Hanging a new peal of bells at the Church of St Bartholome and All Saints, Wootton Basset in 1890. The original bells datec from 1633, but the tower had be come derelict and to commem orate Queen Victoria's Jubilee treble bell and a new second and third were added to the pea and a Guild of Ringers was formed.

46. (*Opposite*) Women weaving a carpet on a hand-loom at the Royal Wilton Carpet Factory, in about 1890. They woul sing as they wove. The boxes alongside the women contain tufts of wool, whilst above them the design of the carpet is drawn on pieces of paper. T company was forced to stop using hand-looms in 1955 because of increased costs.

45. Suffragettes speaking outsi The Bear Hotel Chippenham i about 1912. Women obtained the vote in 1918, but up until war broke out meetings such these often resulted in violenc

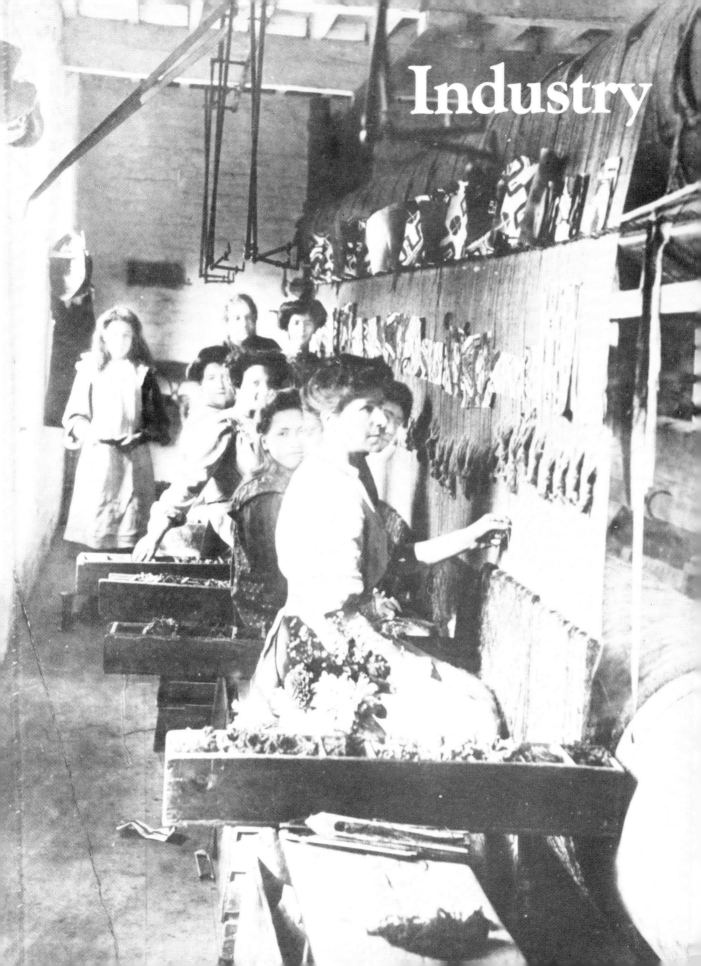

Industry

47. Sam Guley, Alfred Redman, and Charles Park beside the loom for weaving coir doormats at C. W. Maggs's Melksham works. The three men had worked at Maggs's for a total of 168 years when this photograph was taken in 1906.

48. Craftsmen warping the yarn at C. W. Maggs's Melksham rope walk in about 1900. The company was founded in 1802 to manufacture ropes for coalpit cage haulage, and went on to make canvas, corduroy and doormats.

49. A woman operating a loom at one of Trowbridge's ten woollen mills, some time towards the end of the 19th century. The movement of the industry into the small towns of western Wiltshire was due to the invention of the fulling mill. The cloth was felted together in a solution of water and fuller's earth, which was in turn pounded by heavy hammers driven by water.

50. Seend Iron Works during the construction of the uncompleted blast furnaces in 1860. Started in 1857 and finally dismantled in 1889, the Great Western Iron Ore, Smelting & Coal Company was dogged by ill-fortune, speculators, and the bankruptcy of each of the six companies who controlled the works. One of the promoters, an enterprising Devizes bank manager, bought some of the land for £500 and then sold it to his own company for £2,500. All that remains of this spectacular failure are the quarries and part of the connecting railway embankment.

51. The bacon curing room at C. & T. Harris's Calne factory in about 1900. The company's rise began in the late 18th century when John Harris opened a butcher's shop in the town. Calne was then on the route for Irish pigs being driven from Bristol to London, and his sons were able to build up a small curing business. In 1847 when supplies began to fail because of the Irish potato famine, one of the brothers went to America and returned to Calne having seen ice-cooled curing houses at work. In 1864 Harris's took out a patent for an ice-room; using both imported Norwegian ice and local canal ice the company was able to cure bacon throughout the summer as well as in winter. Harris's future was assured, and by 1900 the company was slaughtering two thousand pigs a week and producing a mile and a half of sausages a day.

52. Harry Beak inside the malthouse of the Cross Hayes Brewery, Malmesbury in about 1880. At one time the town boasted three breweries and thirty-two pubs.

Children

54. Teffont children playing in a field known as the 'Gason' in about 1895. They may have been playing any one of a host of traditional village green games such as 'Here Come Three Tinkers', 'Thread the Tailor's Needle', and 'Green Gravel'.

53. Children gathered in the road by a fallen tree on the outskirts of Amesbury in about 1900.

55. A group of boys outside the Fives Court at Marlborough College in 1885. The school had been founded in 1843 for the sons of professional people, especially clergymen, on 'economical terms'. After an uncertain start, culminating in 1851 with a state of almost open warfare between staff and boys, the College gradually became one of the most respected of Victorian public schools.

56. Shaw House School near Melksham in about 1870.

57. The pupils of Melksham Lowbourne British School in 1902. The headmaster was Thomas George, and *Kelly's Directory* for the year notes that although 330 children were registered, average daily attendance seldom exceeded 225.

The Gentry

59. A group of people, Fox Talbot's wife possibly amongst them, in the gardens at Lacock Abbey, their family home since the 16th century, in the early 1840s.

58. (*Overleaf*) The occupants of 17 The Close, Salisbury, gathered in the back garden in 1890.

61. A calotype by Fox Talbot of two people in the grounds of Lacock Abbey in 1844.

60. Edward VII and Queen Alexandra leaving Bowood House, the home of the Marquess of Lansdowne, before visiting Calne in July 1907. The main building no longer exists and only the Diocletian Wing (to the extreme left of the photograph), which was based on the Bishop's Palace at Spalato, Yugoslavia, still stands.

62. Dr Jeston and his wife sitting in 1880 in the garden at Tower House, Malmesbury, with his assistant Dr Kinnair and the domestic staff. Dr Jeston was the Public Vaccinator and a member of the Board of Guardians.

63. The daughters of Dr Taylor playing what appears to be a mixture of bowls and croquet in the gardens of Alkerton House, Cricklade, 1902.

64. The 4th Marquess and the Marchioness of Bath outside Longleat in August 1884 with four of their children. Left to right they are: Lord John Thynne, killed in a riding accident in 1887, Lord Alexander Thynne, killed in action in 1918, and Lady Katherine and Lady Beatrice Thynne.

65. The four children of the 14th Earl of Pembroke in a landau outside Wilton House in 1897. From left to right they are: Lord George Herbert, Lord Reginald Herbert, and Lady Muriel and Lady Beatrix Herbert. Wyatt's Gothic windows were removed by Lord Reginald shortly after he succeeded to the title in 1913.

The Market~Place

66. (*Overleaf*) Queen Victoria's Golden Jubilee being celebrated in the Cross Hayes Malmesbury in 1887. That it was a boiling hot day is indicated by the number of parasols and umbrellas in use. Note also the band playing, and the hogsheads of ale mounted in carts.

67. An early photograph of Salisbury Market taken in about 1860. Because of the cheaper timber and lower rents and wages in the county, waggons made in Wiltshire were responsible for keeping the price down nationally. In 1860 a four-wheeled waggon would have cost about £30, or a year's wages for a farm labourer.

68. Salisbury's Tuesday Cattle Market in about 1890. Notice how organised and tidy the Market has become in the 30 years that separate the two photographs. Note the line of poultry and rabbit hutches. The Market was run by two firms of auctioneers, and temporary pens and hurdles were erected every week.

69. Cricklade cattle market in progress in the High St. in about 1890.

70. Wootton Bassett market in 1907. The 'Great Monthly Cattle Market' was started in 1836 when the town lost its right as a 'Rotten Borough' to elect M.P.s, and thus a major source of its income. On the first market 772 beasts, 32 horses, 487 sheep, and 153 pigs were sold. Fat cattle fetched 10s. a score, mutton 6d. a lb., barley 36s. a quarter, cheese 60s. a cwt., butter 10½d. a lb., eggs 24 for 1s., and ducks and poultry from 2s. 6d. a couple. In the September market the records note that: 'A fine specimen of Cox's New Imperial Swedish Turnip was exhibited by Mr Collins of Sutton Benger, which attracted great attention for its beauty and unusually large size'. The success of the market inspired its organisers to start two Hiring Fairs in 1837, at one of which 400 people were engaged in work for a year. If at the end of that year the labourer or domestic's work had been satisfactory, he or she was presented with a length of material or a hat. The Hiring Fair lost popularity with the arrival of cheap advertisement columns in local papers, and the market in Wootton Bassett High St. was closed in 1939 because it did not comply with the sanitary regulations.

⌂ 71. At the public dinner in the Market Square, Salisbury, to celebrate the Coronation of Edward VII in 1902, 250 carvers
⌂ between them carved 2 tons of meat for 4,000 people. The following comes from the *Salisbury Journal*: 'The carvers and Meat Committee were photographed in front of the council chamber, and the mayor was presented with a set of carvers'.

⌂ 72. A view of Salisbury's public dinner. 4,000 men ate 1,600 lb. of pudding and drank 800 gallons of beer. In the afternoon 4,000 women ate a ton of cake and drank 50 lb. of tea. 'The whole of the catering was carried out by Mr Salter, and that everything was admirably done could be judged from the many expressions of satisfaction that were heard.'

3. Swindon's General Market on
Saturday in 1905. The market
in Commercial Rd. was opened
in 1892 at a cost to the corporation of £4,500, and covered in
1903. The market had space for
7 shops and 80 stalls.

4. Queen Victoria's Diamond
Jubilee celebration in the Square,
Wilton, 1897, before the demoli-
tion of the Wool Loft. The following is from the *Salisbury
Journal*: 'The square looked ex-
ceedingly pretty, festoons of
fairy lamps hanging between the
whole of the trees. The celebration itself took place on Thursday, and commenced with a dinner in the market place at noon.
This was for persons over fourteen, and passed off most suc-
cessfully despite the heat'.

Country Crafts

76. Digging a dewpond shortly after 1900. On the right is Charles White of Imber, chief dew pond maker to the Ecclesiastical Commissione Dewponds were dug on the chalk downs to pr vide watering places for the flocks of wanderi sheep. They were dug to a depth of about ten feet in the middle, and made watertight with layer of clay beaten hard and covered with lir This was in turn followed with a layer of whe straw and finally a layer of earth. The term 'dewpond' is misleading because the ponds ac ally filled with rainwater, and overnight dew would have done little more than compensate for evaporation.

75. (Overleaf) The blacksmith Aenos Maynard shoeing a horse at Easterton Forge in about 19 When Joseph Gye bought the smithy in 1910 he paid 1s. for the grindstone, 23s. for the anvil and block, 2 guineas for the bellows, anc 10s. for the blacksmith's platform – used for binding wheels, and on which the little boy is standing.

77. Bill King outside his Saddlers and Harness Makers shop in Wootton Bassett High St. in 1

78. A flint-knapper at work near Salisbury shortly after the turn of the century. The knapper is retouching the end of one of many long thin flakes known as blades taken from the core of flint, before breaking it into short lengths for use as gunflints. Note the little tubs of prepared flints, and both the bucket and lamp.

79. Joseph Gye's wheelwright and carpenter's yard in Market Lavington, 1906. Milk floats such as the one in the foreground were sold for about £5. When James Gye, the founder of this small Wiltshire family firm, was apprenticed in 1854, he was paid 1s. a week for the first year rising to 5s. in his fifth and final year.

81. Edward Boulter's Wootton Bassett brick-works in 1898. Most towns had their own brick-works, and in this photograph the brickmaster is moulding bricks before they are barrowed under shelter and allowed to dry out. After dry-ing, up to 30,000 bricks were burnt in either a clamp or kiln. Moulds were made of wood and were a standard 9 by 4½ by 3 inches.

82. Women with their spindle wheels outside the Stonehenge Woollen Industry shop in Lake-cum-Wilsford, near Amesbury, in 1898. The indus-try was started by Catherine Lovibond (whose family owned Lake House) for women out-workers on the Estate.

80. Thomas Russ the boot and shoe maker, who had a room at the back of Silas Riddick's boot and shoe warehouse in Wootton Bassett at the turn of the century.

COTTELL BROT...

COTTELL BROS
OPTICIANS
GILDERS
AND
PLATERS.

SILVERSMITHS

Tradesmen

83. (*Overleaf*) Cottell Bros., Jewellers and Opticians, of Regent St., Swindon in about 1900.

86. Chapman's China, Glass & Staffordshire Warehouse, Trowbridge, in 1873.

84. A baker standing outside his premises near Devizes in about 1900. In his left hand the baker holds a wooden oven peel used for drawing loaves from the oven.

85. The Bowood Coach after it had been cleaned, painted, and re-upholstered for the visit of King Edward and Queen Alexandra to Calne, outside Harper's Coach & Motor Works in July 1907.

87. Dodge Brothers' Boot Store, Fleet St., Swindon in 1910. Prices range from slippers at 1s. 6d. a pair to men's boots at about 5s.

88. Hooper the photographer outside his Cromwell Rd., Swindon premises in 1912.

89. F. Sparkes, a Regent St., Swindon butcher's shop in 1887. Rib of beef was 8d. a lb. and brisket 3d.; note the number of rabbits for sale.

90. Henry Lawrence in the backyard of The Cross Keys, Wootton Bassett, of which he was licensee in 1899. In common with many publicans whose trade was small Lawrence had other occupations: he was also a blacksmith and sub-postman. Here he can be seen in his postman's uniform before setting out to collect the mail from Swindon.

91. Pain & Sons' Castle St. Brewery, Salisbury, in about 1875. The site is now a supermarket.

The Military

93. N.C.O.s and men of the Wiltshire Volunteers in 1868. The Volunteers were raised in 1859 following the Indian Mutiny and after an unorthodox seven years during which time at least one unit, raised by Earl St Maur and consisting mostly of farmers, managed to combine drill with fox-hunting, the Volunteers settled down into two thousand-man Battalions commanded by General Buckley who had fought as a subaltern at Waterloo in 1815.

92. (*Overleaf*) The Royal Flying Corps training on Salisbury Plain in August 1912. That month a reporter from the *Sphere* visited the aerodrome and after commenting on the inadequacies of the monoplane compared to the French or German biplane, went on: 'On Friday of last week there were no fewer than ten flyers in the air at one time soaring, swooping, and wheeling in all directions, while the air was full of the droning hum of their engines.'

95. Officers of the 1st Battalion the Wiltshire
Rifle Volunteers. In the centre is Major the Earl
of Pembroke, and on his right the commanding
officer, Colonel Everett. This photograph was
probably taken in 1881 before the Battalion set
off for a Review at Windsor of 52,000 troops by
Queen Victoria. The problems of feeding these
numbers were immense, and a history of the
Volunteers published in 1887 has the following
to say: 'Quarter Master Fawcett hired a medium
sized furniture van in which beer, wine, bread,
cheese, pasties of pig's flesh (said to be) for about
a thousand individuals were stowed away, the
pasties making were the night's work for half
the cooks at Salisbury.'

94. Lord Roberts inspecting a motorised military
unit in Marlborough in 1903. Most famous for
his defeat of the Afghans at Kandahar, and for
the relief of Mafeking during the Boer War,
Lord Roberts was Commander-in-Chief until 1904.

96 and 97. These two photographs show the development of the Royal Wiltshire Militia during the late 19th and early 20th centuries. The Napoleonic flavour of the Marlborough troop of the Militia in 1875 is somewhat incongruous when compared to the officers of the 3rd Battalion, the Wiltshire Regiment (Duke of Edinburgh's) at Devizes in 1909. The Battalion was formed in 1908 out of the Militia as a reserve force to provide drafts for the regular Army, and during the Great War the Battalion provided over 13,000 men for the Wiltshire Regiment overseas. Note that fourteen out of the eighteen officers have moustaches.

98. W. J. Carter of Cricklade, an officer in the Royal Wiltshire Yeomanry in 1890. The *Rules & Regulations* issued in 1877 list the cost of much of Carter's uniform: tunic £1 15s. 6d., shako and plume 10s. 6d., spurs 1s. 6d., scabbard 4s. 6d., and sword 17s.

99. The Square, Mere, in 1908. The following extract comes from the *Salisbury Journal* of 8 August: 'On Wednesday morning the inhabitants of Mere were asked to witness the passing through the town of three battalions of troops, consisting of the Rifle Brigade, the 2nd Devons, and the 2nd Somerset Light Infantry, and also a detachment of the Army Service Corps with baggage'.

100. A transport unit of the Supply Corps at Bulford Camp in 1909.

Three battalions of troops under the command of General Grover camped at Ashwell, then
ut a mile out of Mere, in August 1908. Note the Ind Coope brewery waggon on the right.

W. E. Chivers & Sons, the Devizes contractors, transporting Canadian military equipment at Bulford Camp in the autumn of 1914.

The Railways

103. (*Overleaf*) Some of the 197 engines, 555 carriages, and 3,260 waggons in the 15 miles of sidings that comprised the Great Western Railway 'mortuary' at Swindon after the passing of the Broad Gauge in May 1892. The death of the Broad Gauge had been inevitable since its acceptance by the G.W.R. in 1838, but *Punch* lamented its passing with a cartoon depicting an engine with the shades of its greatest disciples, Isambard Kingdom Brunel and Sir Daniel Gooch, looking on, and the following poem in imitation of 'The Burial of Sir John Moore':
'Not a whistle was heard, not a brass bell note,
As his corse o'er the sleepers we hurried.
Not a fog signal wailed from a husky throat
O'er the grave where our Broad Gauge we buried.'

104. A Broad Gauge engine in the 1880s. The gauge was seven foot wide which was sufficient to allow for 'dining and sleeping salons and other luxuries as could be obtained at West End Clubs. The controversy between supporters of the two gauges was both bitter and emotional as can be realised by the following epitaph of a G.W.R. driver:
'When Narrow with Broad first began to entwine
A grey headed driver was killed on the line,
His last feeble whisper was caught by his mate –
"Thank God t'was broad gauge where I met with my Fate".'

105. A general view of the Great Western Railway works at Swindon in the 1880s. On the right is the Medical Fund Swimming Bath. Swindon was a small market town with a population of 2,000 when the Great Western's chief engineer, Brunel, chose it as a major repair depot for the company in 1841. The town was ideally situated along the network of valleys between Bristol and London, with their gentle gradients for trains, and had easy access to the South Wales coalfields via the canal network.

106. Cricklade Station in 1885. The line, on the Midland & South Western Junction Railway, opened in December 1883 with celebrations in The White Hart and a fireworks display. The return fare to London was 8s.

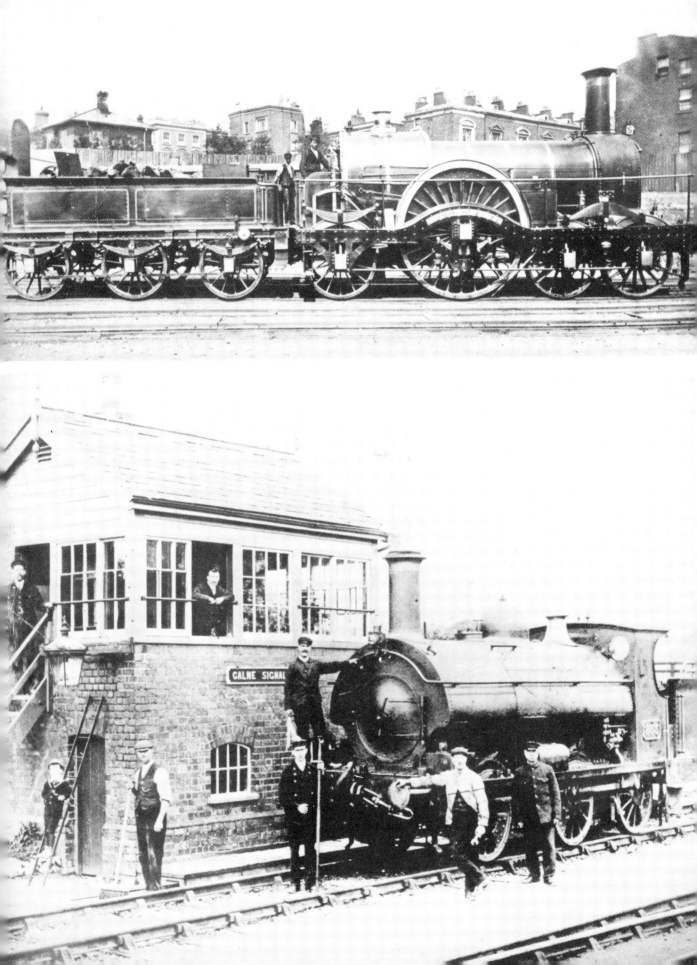

107. *Lord of the Isles*. Perhaps the best known of all the Broad Gauge engines built at Swindon by the Great Western Railway, the Courier Class *Lord of the Isles* was exhibited at the Great Exhibition in 1851, and withdrawn from service in 1884 having run 780,000 miles with the same boiler.

109. The Great Western Railway's Annual Outing in 1910. The company built a Mechanics Institute, a theatre, dance-hall, schools and churches for its employees; and also founded the Medical Fund Society which provided free medical treatment.

108. Great Western Railway engine No. 853 outside Calne Signal Box in about 1900. The Calne Railway Company was founded in 1863 by a group of town businessmen who put up the money to build a branch line from Chippenham. The Great Western Railway ran the service on licence until 1892 when they bought control of the Company. The line was closed in 1965.

110. Inside the welding shop at the Great Western Railway's Swindon Works in about 1900. With about 9,000 employees the company cou produce a locomotive a week, a carriage a day and a waggon every hour. Apart from the wel ing shop there was also a fitting shop, leather shop, sewing shop, carriage building departmen carpentery shop, wheelwright's shop, brass works, foundry, boiler shop, paint shop, road waggon shop, and french polishing departmen

111. The construction crew of the Great Weste Railway's Malmesbury branch line gathered round the 'coffee pot', an engine used for haul ing railway sleepers and hardcore out to the si in 1876, the year before the line was opened.

112. The Great Western Railway Stores Department boarding charabancs for their annual summer outing in June 1909 to Newton Abbot, Moretonhampstead and Becky Falls.

113. Workers crossing Emlyn Square after leaving the Great Western Railway works in Swindon in 1906. Houses for the employees were built at the company's expense with small front gardens and a backyard containing a wash-house and privy. Because Swindon was virtually a one-industry town its social life was based on the definite hierarchy of the railway works. In 1908 foremen were paid 70s. a week, and most other workers 33s.

Farming and Forestry

114. (*Overleaf*) Pausing for refreshment whilst haymaking at the Lush's Highland Farm, West Lavington, in 1900. Haymaking and harvesting were the two times in the year when the women and children went out into the fields to help their menfolk. Note the oxen to the right.

115. A woodman, possibly one of the Pike brothers, in Amesbury Park, the home of Sir Edmund Antrobus, in the summer of 1902.

116. Two dung carts on a farm near Devizes in about 1900. Agricultural wages before the Great War were 12s. a week with a cottage; and even a medium-sized farm would have employed a foreman, carters, shepherds, ploughmen, dairymen, a groom-gardener, labourers, and innumerable boys and lads all earning about 5s.

7. The miller Abraham Lock standing outside Blackland Mill, near Calne on the river Marden, in 1903.

8. Jack Dunford resting from gathering stones for road-mending near Teffont in about 1895. The two meals of the farm labourers' working day were 'nunch' or breakfast, and 'nammet' which was eaten at noon. Note the 'yorked' corduroy trousers, the can of cold tea, and the wicker basket – often a temporary home for the odd poached rabbit!

119. A team of oxen at work on Maundrell's Farm, Morgan's Hill Calstone, near Calne in 1908. Oxen were gradually replaced as equipment became lighter and heavy horse breeds improved.

121. Threshing near Wootton Bassett in about 1890. The following description of Wiltshire threshing is from A. G. Street's *Farmer's Glory*: 'It was hard work. There was a balanced team of men to run the outfit. Two men pitched the sheaves onto the top of the thresher, where one man cut the strings and another fed the grain steadily and smoothly into the machine. Two men made the straw rick, one took off the chaff, and one the grain, whilst Tom the driver was in charge of the machinery. Any one slackening speed could slow up the whole business. No extra money was paid to the regular-farming men for threshing, but beer was allowed on threshing days, one quart per man.' The arrival of Burrell's stationary engine and the threshing machine in the mid-19th century had put paid to winter threshing with flails in a barn. The machine could complete 8 men's work for 6 months in 10 days, and was the cause of much grumbling about unemployment when it first appeared on the market.

120. Gathering the corn sheaves at harvest time on Robert Hooper's Cornbury Farm, West Lavington, in about 1904. The carter's day would have begun at 6 a.m. and finished at 8 in the evening. Once the last rick had been built the men would have gathered in a barn for the annual harvest supper. After eating three courses, liberally washed down with ale, the men would help themselves to bowls of shag provided by the farmer. There would have been speeches and songs and the men would have returned home at about ten o'clock after singing 'God Save the King'.

122. George Ford, the shepherd at Stonehenge, standing on the Winterbourne Stoke road in 1901, the year Stonehenge was fenced in.

123. The Aldbourne team of sheepshearers in about 1904. Local contract teams of shearers existed throughout Wiltshire during the 19th century, and in the case of the Aldbourne team the two leaders would go to Swindon market a month before shearing time and book shearing dates with local farmers.

24. The woodmen at Lacock from a calotype by Fox Talbot about 1842. Up until the introduction of a now universal American-designed axe in the middle of the 19th century all woodmen used the straight-handled, iron-headed, wedge-shaped axe being used in this photograph.

25. A team of horses hauling timber through Rowde in about 1900. The logs were cross-hauled up a short ramp on to the bed of the pole waggon by the horses working from the further side of the carriage: a method well suited to scattered work and requiring no special tackle.

▷ 128. (*Opposite*) Chippenham Cycling Club gathered outside James Perkins's Wine and Spirit Vaults in 1910.

◁ 126. A rural scene near Lacock in about 1842, from a calotype by Fox Talbot. The five-bar gate and quantity of timber suggest this may have been a local carpenter's yard.

◁ 127. A farm labourer returning home to his cottage at the end of a day's work in the fields near Devizes, in about 1900. Having eaten tea would have probably put in an hour's work in the allotment before going down to the local and spending part of his week's pocket-money on a half pint of 1½d. beer.

Transport

WILLIAM? BREWERY LIMITED'S ENTIRE.

WINE & SPIRIT VAULTS

PERKINS

JAMES PERKINS
WINE AND SPIRIT
MERCHANT

⌂ 129. The very popular Joe Osmond who ran the hansom cab rank outside Salisbury Railway Station in about 1900.

131. The Warminster Motor Company Works in George St., Warminster, in 1904. The garage was started by a consortium of local gentry, including the Marquess of Bath and the Duke of Somerset, in order that they might get their cars serviced and repaired. The front right hand car is a 12 h.p. Napier, and that behind it an 8 h.p. Beaufort.

132. Enos Cowley in his first car outside his Cycle Works in the Square, Mere, in about 1905.

130. A Scout bus belonging to Hall & Sons' Orcheston-based Shrewton Motor Services in 1914 This private carrier service ran from Tilshead via Shrewton to the Market Square, Salisbury, and caused something of a local revolution when it first started in 1912. The Salisbury Scout Motor Company which was founded in 1902 by the Burden brothers was the only attempt by a Wiltshire company to manufacture motor cars. By 1912 the company was producing two vehicles a week and employing 150 men. They made cars up to rally standard and the speed record for a Scout car was 52.9 m.p.h. The company went out of production in 1921, and today only two of their cars still exist.

133. Two barges, one of them the *Caroline*, at the bottom of the seventeen locks that comprised the Caen Hill flight of the Kennet & Avon canal at Devizes, in the 1880s. The flight took three hours to ascend, and along with the Devizes Steps (a further eleven locks) rose 239 feet in 2⅞ miles. The canal was unable to compete with the railways and never made a profit on trade goods after 1877. Note the horse on the tow-path.

4. A Four-in-Hand Rally in
Chippenham in about 1906.

5. An omnibus of the Bath
Electric Tramways outside The
Kings Arms Hotel, Melksham,
about 1912.

136. Monsieur Salmet, 'the intrepid flyer', refuelling the first plane to land in Swindon, in July 1912. A contemporary account of Salmet's visit to the town said that after refuelling, 'the aviator was able to volplane, switchback, circle, and draw figures in the air at will. He darted over the heads of the people for twenty minutes. They laughed and cheered themselves hoarse'.

137. The airship *Beta* at Alderbury, near Salisbury, in September 1910. The *Beta* was forced down with a burst carburettor whilst taking part in the largest military manoeuvres the country had ever known. Involving 48,000 troops divided into two armies and superintended by the Commander-in-Chief, Sir John French, the final 'battle' on Salisbury Plain was watched by the Duke of Connaught, Churchill (then Home Secretary), Kitchener, Lord Roberts, and most of an elegant and large house party staying at Wilton House with Lord Pembroke especially for the occasion. The manoeuvres are of note in that they mark the first time an aeroplane was ever used for military scouting.

138. Miss Stratton on a tricycle at Melksham in about 1890. The tricycle cost ten guineas, and an advertisement in a 19th century directory stated: 'The tricycle is specially adapted for Clergymen, Ministers, Doctors, Surveyors, Inland Revenue Officers, Ladies or Gentlemen needing moderate and healthful recreation, and for all who are not inclined to undertake the expense of horse, carriage, and servant'.

139. R. Horton, a Burbage butcher, in his three-wheeler delivery van in about 1912.

140. Rex motorcycles outside Stratton's Repair Works, Melksham, in 1904.

143. (*Opposite*) A woman holding a besom brush outside her Fisherton de le Mare cottage in 1913. Note the canary cage to the top right of the door. Besoms were made with bundles of birch twigs that had been cut in winter and allowed to season, and they were then tied to lime handles with thin strips of oak, ash or lime.

141. Charlie Ferris, licensee of The Lamb at Rowde, Devizes in his trap outside the inn in about 1900.

142. A six-ton Wotton engine delivering a new boiler to a Chippenham cloth factory in about 1890.

Scenes from Wiltshire Life

144. Walter Laurence with his wife and sisters in his garden at Aldbourne in about 1900. Laurence was a land-measurer, sign-writer, painter and decorator. Known as 'Tapey' because of his affection for measuring, one of his jobs was to throw a weighted tape over freshly thatched cottages to ensure that the thatcher had not overcharged for the area thatched.

46. A labourer with his wife and
six children outside their cottage
near Devizes in about 1900.

145. A gipsy family, the Mollarts, near Warminster in 1904. Until
the army occupation of much of Salisbury Plain in 1900 it was a
favourite grazing area for gipsies – and the following poem ex-
plains why:
'Oh! Salisbury Plain is bleak and bare,
At least, so I've heard many people declare,
For I fairly confess I never was there.
Not a shrub or a tree,
Not a bush you can see.
No hedges, no ditches, no gates, no stiles,
Much less a cottage or house for miles '

147. A meet of the Vale of the White Horse Hunt outside the Beaufort Brewery, Wootton Bassett, in about 1890. There was much argument as to who should hunt the better coverts in North Wiltshire when the Beaufort Hunt relinquished control over much of its traditional territory, and new and independent hunts were started. The Vale of the White Horse Hunt was founded in 1886, and by 1910 was hunting three days a week and killing about sixty brace of fox in a season.

148. The Riddick and Easley families back from a blackberrying expedition along the hedgerows round Wootton Bassett in 1900.

9. The vicar of Imber, the
Reverend James Pearson, in a
donkey cart with his garden boy
and housekeeper sometime between 1885 and 1899. The army
occupation of Salisbury Plain
began in 1897 when the War
Office bought sixty square miles
for £450,000. Imber was com-
pulsorily purchased in 1934, and
250 inhabitants were 'tempor-
arily' evacuated in 1943. Since
then most of the village has
been destroyed.

10. The Bolingbroke Arms, Hook
about 1860. The woman in the
doorway is probably Mrs Francis
Hitchcock, the licensee, and it is
possible that the men in the trap
are drinking either porter at 1s.
a gallon or light ale at 7d.
a gallon from the Beaufort Brewery, Wootton Bassett.

151. Jim Welch in his 10 h.p. Back Entrance Pipe car, taking volunteers to the station at Mere after the declaration of war in August 1914. The war began on 4 August and that week the headlines in the *Salisbury Journal* announced: 'At seven o'clock on Tuesday evening Great Britain became involved in the greatest war known since the days of Napoleon. The war is not of England's seeking'. It ended on 11 November 1918 after approximately 12 million soldiers and civilians had been killed.